PORTUGAL

By Jennifer Lombardo
and Alicia Z. Klepeis

EXPLORING
WORLD
CULTURES

Cavendish
Square

Published in 2025 by Cavendish Square Publishing, LLC
2544 Clinton Street, Buffalo, NY 14224

Second Edition

Library of Congress Cataloging-in-Publication Data

Names: Lombardo, Jennifer, author. | Klepeis, Alicia, 1971- author.
Title: Portugal / Jennifer Lombardo and Alicia Z. Klepeis.
Description: Second edition. | Buffalo, NY : Cavendish Square Publishing, 2025. | Series: Exploring world cultures | Includes index.
Identifiers: LCCN 2024027423 | ISBN 9781502672858 (library binding) | ISBN 9781502672841 (paperback) | ISBN 9781502672865 (ebook)
Subjects: LCSH: Portugal--Juvenile literature.
Classification: LCC DP517 .K54 2025 | DDC 946.9--dc23/eng/20240809
LC record available at https://lccn.loc.gov/2024027423

Writers: Alicia Z. Klepeis; Jennifer Lombardo (second edition)
Editor: Jennifer Lombardo
Copyeditors: Jill Keppeler and Danielle Haynes
Designer: Deanna Lepovich

The photographs in this book are used by permission and through the courtesy of: Cover Tomsickova Tatyana/Shutterstock.com; p. 4 Mazur Travel/Shutterstock.com; p. 5 artem evdokimov/Shutterstock.com; p. 6 Carla Isabel A Nascimento/Shutterstock.com; p. 7 seamuss/Shutterstock.com; p. 8 Tatohra/Shutterstock.com; p. 9 Ryan_hoel/Shutterstock.com; p. 10 Zoran Karapancev/Shutterstock.com; p. 11 Alexandros Michailidis/Shutterstock.com; p. 12 Oleg Znamenskiy/Shutterstock.com; p. 13 (main) PIXEL to the PEOPLE/Shutterstock.com; p. 13 (inset) barmalini/Shutterstock.com; p. 15 (top) Jesus Cobaleda/Shutterstock.com; p. 15 (bottom) Vitaly Fedotov/Shutterstock.com; p. 16 Radiokafka/Shutterstock.com; p. 17 De Visu/Shutterstock.com; p. 18 Sean Hsu/Shutterstock.com; p. 19 DaLiu/Shutterstock.com; p. 20 Analisisgadgets/Shutterstock.com; p. 21 Sergey Zuenok/Shutterstock.com; p. 22 Go My Media/Shutterstock.com; p. 23 Pantuna/Shutterstock.com; p. 24 Lina Balciunaite/Shutterstock.com; p. 25 iacomino FRiMAGES/Shutterstock.com; p. 26 Tatiana Popova/Shutterstock.com; p. 27 (main) Rui Alexandre Araujo/Shutterstock.com; p. 27 (inset) Stefan Constantin 22/Shutterstock.com; p. 28 JM Travel Photography/Shutterstock.com; p. 29 Nitr/Shutterstock.com.

CPSIA compliance information: Batch #CW25CSQ: For further information contact Cavendish Square Publishing LLC at 1-877-980-4450.

Printed in the United States of America

CONTENTS

INTRODUCTION

People have lived in the European country of Portugal for thousands of years. For a long time, kings ruled the country. Today, Portugal is a **democracy**. The leader of the country is called the prime minister.

People in Portugal have many kinds of jobs. Some work in hotels, hospitals, or schools. Others make cars or catch fish from the sea. Portuguese farmers grow many types of food on their land.

There are many beautiful old buildings in Portugal.

Tourists and Portuguese alike enjoy visiting Portugal's many beaches.

Portugal has beaches, mountains, and forests. Tourists, or visitors, come from around the world to learn about Portugal's history and see its lovely sights.

Like all countries, Portugal has its share of problems. **Racism** and **climate** change are two problems that affect many countries, including Portugal. Portugal also has a housing problem. There are not enough houses for everyone, and the ones that are available are getting too expensive for the Portuguese to afford. The government has promised to work on these problems to help the Portuguese.

GEOGRAPHY

Portugal is a little smaller than the U.S. state of Indiana. The country covers 35,556 square miles (92,090 square kilometers).

Portugal is located on the Iberian Peninsula in western Europe. It shares a border with one other country: Spain, to Portugal's east. The Atlantic Ocean is to the west. The Gulf of Cádiz lies to its south. The climate is rainy and cool in the north but warmer and drier in the south.

FACT!

"Serra da Estrela" means "Mountain of the Star" in Portuguese.

The Rio Tejo, or Tagus River, begins in Spain and runs through Portugal. It empties into the Atlantic Ocean.

Mountains and **plateaus** make up much of northern Portugal. The country's highest mountain range is called the Serra da Estrela. There are many plains and rolling hills in southern Portugal.

This map shows where Portugal is in the world.

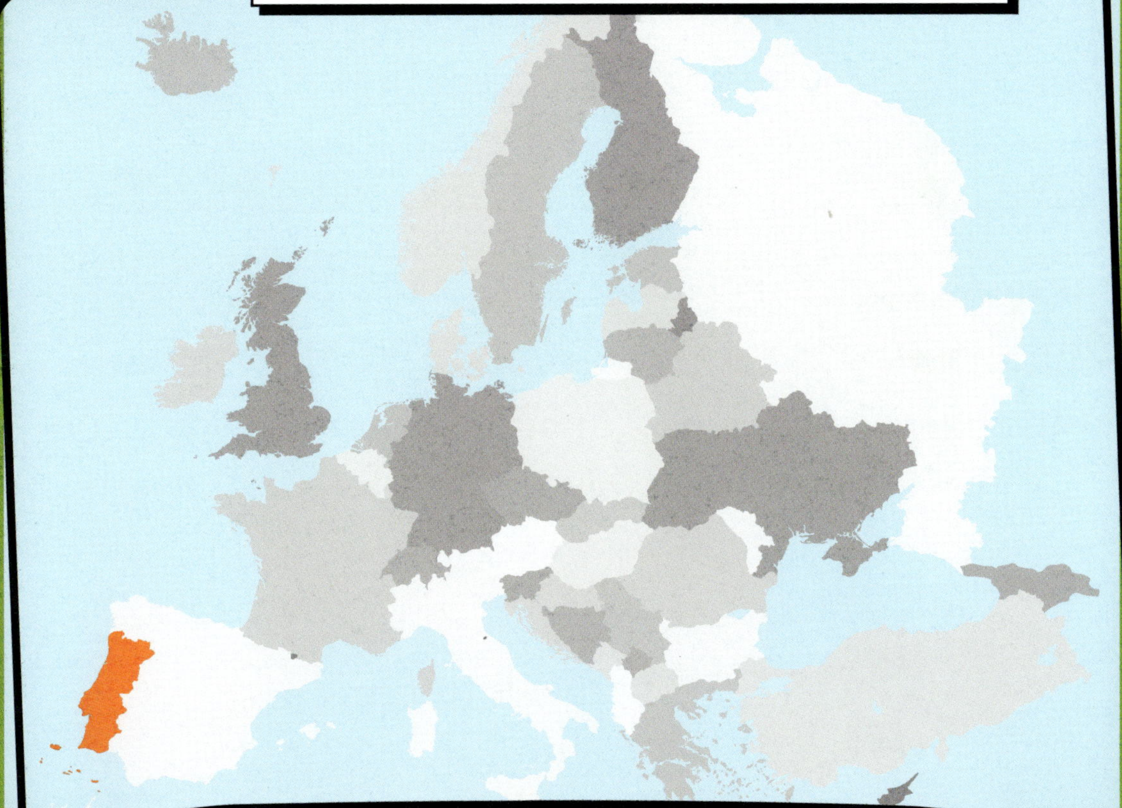

PORTUGAL'S EXTRA LANDS

Portugal controls two archipelagos, or groups of islands. The Azores lie west of Portugal in the Atlantic Ocean. The Madeira islands are off the northwest coast of Africa.

HISTORY

During the 700s CE, people from North Africa (often called the Moors) arrived in what is now Portugal and took control. They also brought new foods, art forms, and styles of architecture, or building, to Portugal.

The Christians who were already living in Portugal fought the Moors. In 1139, Portugal became an independent monarchy, or a country ruled by a king. Starting in the 1400s, Portuguese explorers set out on trips all over the world. Over time, Portugal created colonies in Africa, South America, and Asia.

Portugal's flag was designed in 1910, when the country first became a democracy.

The Palace of Queluz was one of the homes of the Portuguese royal family. Today, tourists can pay to see it.

FACT!

Portugal's current **constitution** was written in 1976, soon after the country became a democracy again.

In 1910, Portugal changed from a monarchy to a democracy. Then, starting in 1932, Portugal became a **dictatorship**. The Portuguese overthrew this government in 1974 and created a democracy again.

THE SLAVE TRADE

Portuguese explorers kidnapped African people and sold them into slavery around the world. Today, the Portuguese generally ignore the problems early explorers caused. Many say they are proud of their history.

GOVERNMENT

Portugal's government has three parts, or branches: legislative, judicial, and executive. In Portugal, the legislative branch is called the Assembly of the Republic. The 230 people who are elected to the Assembly write new laws.

FACT!

The Council of Ministers is made up of the heads of different departments. For example, the minister of education oversees Portugal's schools.

São Bento Palace is in the capital city of Lisbon. It is where the Assembly of the Republic meets.

The courts make up the judicial branch. They follow the country's constitution to decide how the laws should be carried out. The president, prime minister, and Council of Ministers make up the executive branch. They make sure people follow the laws. In Portugal, the president doesn't have much power. Their main job is to be the face of the country. The prime minister is the one who does most of the governing.

In April 2024, Luís Montenegro became prime minister.

CONTROL ON THE RISE

Some Portuguese liked when the country was a dictatorship. They want it to be one again. Many Portuguese citizens are worried about what will happen if these people are elected to government positions.

THE ECONOMY

After the dictatorship ended in 1974, Portugal had a lot of problems with its economy, or the way goods and services were made and sold. The group of countries known as the European Union helped Portugal make changes, and the economy became much stronger. However, now that the country has more money, the government has become less willing to spend it. Citizens have held **protests** about their poor health care and education systems.

Shown here is an olive grove in Portugal.

SERVICE JOBS

About two-thirds of Portuguese workers have service jobs. These include jobs such as hotel workers, teachers, and nurses. Tourism is also a big part of Portugal's economy, so tour guides are in demand.

Portugal's exports, or the items it sells to other countries, have been a big help to its economy. The country's main exports are cars, car parts, and clothes.

Many Portuguese work as fishers and farmers. Olives, grapes, and tomatoes are some of the crops farmers grow.

FACT!

Portugal mainly trades with Spain, Italy, France, and Germany.

Portugal is the world's largest producer of cork items, such as those shown here.

THE ENVIRONMENT

All over the world, governments and individuals are working to make life more **sustainable**. In Portugal, the government has put up solar panels and windmills. These turn energy, or power, from the sun and wind into clean energy, which doesn't pollute the air.

However, Portugal still faces some problems. For example, more than half its garbage goes into landfills. Environmental groups have said the country needs to get better at recycling and **composting**.

Climate change is also causing problems in Portugal. Rising sea levels are an especially big concern because the country has such a long coastline.

A SPECIAL FRUIT

The *pera Rocha*, or Rocha pear, is a kind of pear that grows only in Portugal. The Portuguese enjoy eating it on its own or using it to make desserts and jams.

The Iberian lynx is one animal found in Portugal. There are only a few hundred of these cats left in the world.

FACT!

Portugal and Spain are working together to save the Iberian lynx.

Windmills such as these dot Portugal's countryside.

THE PEOPLE TODAY

Most Portuguese people share a common culture, or way of life. About 94 percent of the people are of Portuguese **ethnicity**. This is a combination of Celtic, Mediterranean, and Arabic ethnicities.

For hundreds of years, Portugal had colonies around the world. Some Africans moved to Portugal as its African colonies gained independence near the end of the 20th century. Since the beginning of the 2000s, most immigrants, or newcomers, have been from Brazil and China.

*Portugal is not very **diverse**. Many of the people look similar to each other.*

Immigrants bring their own beliefs, foods, and languages to Portugal. As the ethnic makeup of the country has changed, many Portuguese have started demanding that the government fight racism.

BRAZIL

Brazil is the biggest country in South America. It was a Portuguese colony for more than 300 years. This is why Brazilians speak Portuguese. The country won its independence in 1822.

FACT!

At the height of its power, Portugal had more than 50 colonies around the world.

Most Portuguese people are very patriotic. This means they love their country.

LIFESTYLE

Nearly 70 percent of Portugal's people live in cities and towns. Some live in houses. Others live in apartments. Families in cities often have computers and cell phones. Some also own cars.

People in Portugal's countryside often lead slower-paced lives than those who live in the city. Some grow crops to eat or to sell. Other farmers raise animals or host tourists at their farms.

FACT!

About 55 percent of Portuguese women today work outside of the home.

Many Portuguese who live in cities use public transportation to get around.

No matter where they live, the Portuguese have some things in common. Family and food tend to be very important to them. Meals are often eaten with family members. The Portuguese also tend to be warm and friendly. They enjoy meeting new people and showing off their country.

CULTURE SHOCK

When a person goes somewhere with different customs than they are used to, they are often surprised and sometimes confused. This is called "culture shock." One thing that may shock Americans is that the Portuguese often greet friends and strangers with a kiss on both cheeks.

Portugal's countryside is quieter and less crowded than its cities.

RELIGION

Portugal has no official religion, or faith. All people are free to follow any religion they want—or no religion at all. However, most people here are Christian. About 85 percent of Portugal's population is Roman Catholic.

Churches are a common sight all over Portugal. Some are hundreds of years old.

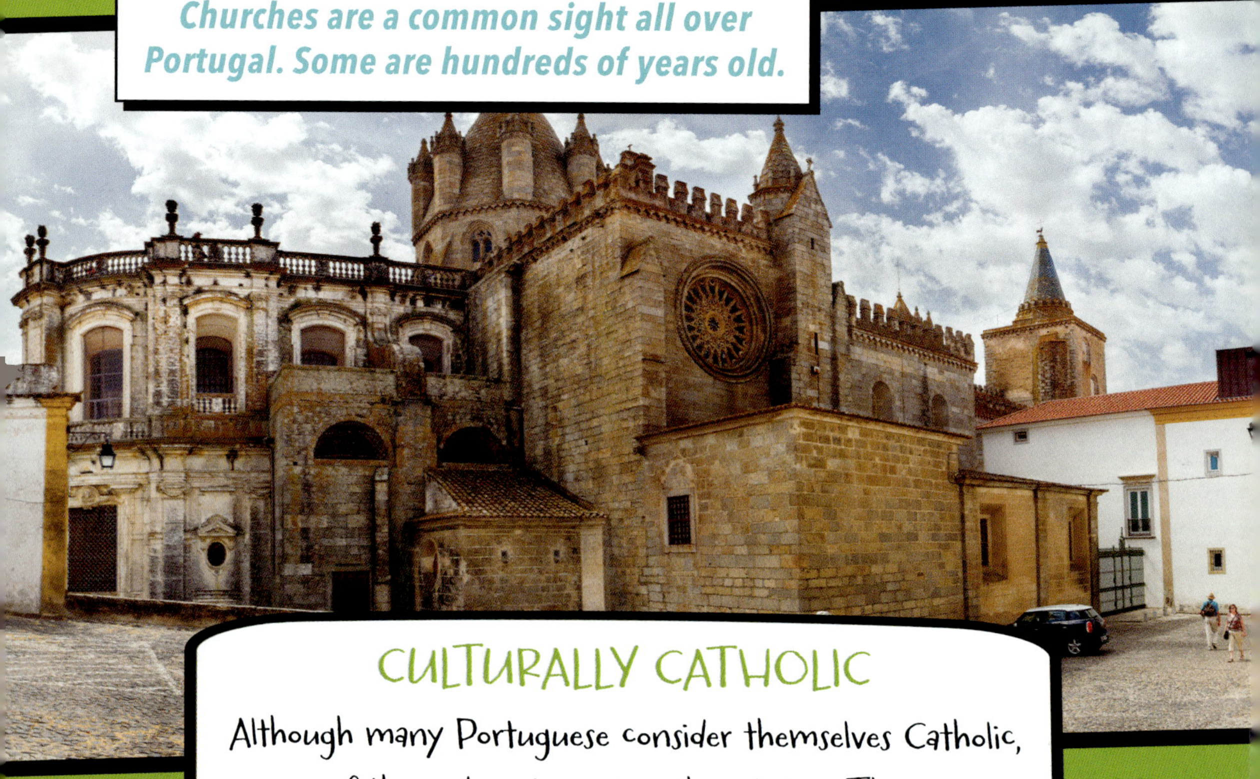

CULTURALLY CATHOLIC

Although many Portuguese consider themselves Catholic, many of them do not practice the religion. This means they don't regularly go to church or follow Catholic teachings, but they may take part in religious celebrations.

Christian church services are held every Sunday in villages and cities across Portugal. Some people attend every week, but many do not. Like other Christians, those in Portugal **celebrate** certain holidays like Easter and Christmas. In the countryside, religious celebrations take place throughout the year. For example, on June 13, Portuguese—especially those who live in Lisbon—celebrate St. Anthony, a Catholic saint.

FACT!

Fewer than 1 percent of Portugal's people follow Judaism, Islam, or another religion other than Christianity.

The Feast of St. Anthony is one of the oldest and most popular celebrations in Lisbon. St. Anthony is the city's ***patron*** *saint.*

LANGUAGE

Portugal's official language is Portuguese. An official language is one used by the government, schools, and businesses. Many people also speak English, but it is not an official language.

Portugal has a second official language called Mirandese. This language only became an official language in 1999. Mirandese is not commonly spoken in Portugal. In fact, only about 15,000 people speak it. Most of them live in the northeast corner of the country.

Portuguese (below) has similarities to Spanish, but the two are different languages.

Portuguese schools commonly teach children English and French. Also, immigrants who come to Portugal from different places may speak languages other than Portuguese. Worldwide, about 250 million people speak Portuguese.

The red part of this map shows where Mirandese is spoken.

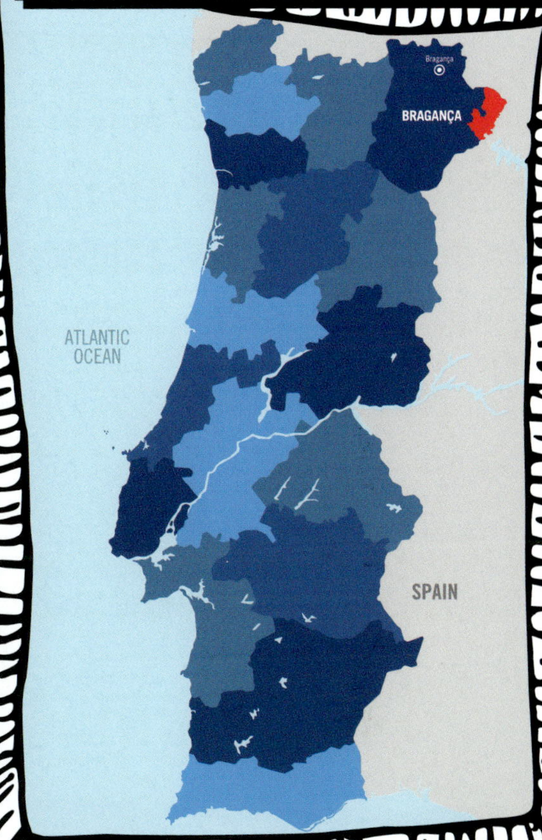

FACT!

Portugal's Deaf community, which numbers about 60,000, uses Portuguese Sign Language.

REGIONAL VS. NATIONAL

Mirandese is an official regional language. This means it is only an official language in certain parts of the country. In contrast, Portuguese is the official national language, meaning it is used everywhere.

ARTS AND FESTIVALS

Like many people around the world, the Portuguese enjoy creating and viewing art. Josefa de Óbidos is a famous Portuguese painter from the 17th century. Her art has been shown in museums around the world.

Music is another important part of Portuguese culture. Fado is a kind of folk music there. People make fado music using stringed instruments known as the *guitarra* and *viola*, and by singing.

FACT!

The Portuguese painting style was heavily **influenced** by Dutch painter Jan van Eyck, who visited Lisbon in the 15th century.

Some festivals are celebrated by wearing special clothes, dancing, and playing music.

Portugal is famous for its beautiful blue and white tiles called* azulejos. *These tiles decorate buildings across the country.

The Portuguese have festivals, or celebrations, throughout the year. Some are national, such as Portugal Day on June 10. Others are smaller, such as the Sintra Festival. This festival, held in the city of Sintra, celebrates classical music.

THE NATIONAL POET

Portugal Day is also called Camões Day after the Portuguese poet Luís Vaz de Camões, who died on June 10, 1580. He has been compared to other famous writers, such as England's William Shakespeare and ancient Greece's Homer.

FUN AND PLAY

Soccer, called *futebol* in Portuguese, is a huge part of Portuguese culture. Basketball is also popular here. Just like in the United States, Portugal has professional soccer and basketball leagues, or groups of teams. With its long coastline, Portugal also offers water sports, including swimming, sailing, and scuba diving.

FACT!
Portuguese people enjoy traveling, both around Portugal and to other countries.

Bullfighting is a part of the culture of Portugal. Some people enjoy it. Others feel the sport is not kind to the animals.

Many Portuguese children enjoy outdoor games such as hopscotch, jump rope, and sack races. In a game called Blind Goat, one person is blindfolded and has to catch the other players as they circle around them. Portuguese kids as well as adults also enjoy playing video games and watching movies.

Soccer fans are known for their strong support of their teams. Cristiano Ronaldo is the best-known Portuguese soccer star.

RELAXATION

Many Portuguese enjoy spending their free time relaxing with friends and family, especially outdoors. They may go to a café, have a picnic in a park, listen to live music, or just take a walk.

FOOD

Portuguese cooks use many spices in their dishes. Cinnamon, pepper, and curry powder are all popular spices here.

Seafood is often on the menu in Portugal. The country's national dish is called *bacalhau*, or salted codfish. There are many different ways to prepare this dish.

FACT!

Relaxing with friends and a cup of coffee is an important part of Portuguese culture.

Seafood and pork feature heavily in Portuguese dishes.

Shown here is a traditional Portuguese dessert: egg pastries and coffee.

People in Portugal also enjoy pork dishes, meaty stews, and soups. It's common to serve meals with potatoes, rice, and salad. Sometimes people eat cheeses before or after a main meal.

For dessert, Portuguese people often eat dishes made with fruit or eggs. A popular rice pudding called *arroz doce* is made with eggs, cinnamon, and lemon.

AN IMPORTED FOOD

Although bacalhau is Portugal's national dish, it did not originally come from Portugal. The country began importing cod in the 14th century from colder countries such as Norway and Iceland. Salting the fish was a way to keep it fresh in Portugal's warm climate.

GLOSSARY

celebrate: To do something special or fun for an important day such as a holiday.

climate: The weather over a long period of time.

composting: Setting aside organic matter to break down and create a mixture that makes land more fertile.

constitution: A document that outlines the basic laws by which a country, state, or group is governed.

democracy: A form of government in which people vote for their leaders.

dictatorship: A form of government in which one person rules a country with total power and often in a harmful way.

diverse: Including many different kinds of people.

ethnicity: A part of a person's identity based on where they or their family come from.

influence: To have an effect on the condition or development of something.

patron: A god or saint that protects a certain place or thing.

plateau: A large area of land with raised sides and a level top.

protest: An event in which people gather to show they do not like something.

racism: The practice of treating others poorly because they are part of a different race, or group of people who look alike in certain ways.

sustainable: Able to last a long time; often used to describe efforts to protect the environment, or natural world.

FIND OUT MORE

Books

Allen, Jules. *Portugal vs. Spain*. North Mankato, MN: Capstone Press, 2023.

Daly-Weir, Catherine. *What Was the Age of Exploration?* New York, NY: Penguin Workshop, 2021.

Dickmann, Nancy. *Your Passport to Portugal*. North Mankato, MN: Capstone Press, 2024.

Websites

Kiddle: Portugal Facts for Kids
kids.kiddle.co/Portugal
Read more about Portugal, and take a look at some amazing pictures.

***National Geographic Kids*: Portugal**
kids.nationalgeographic.com/geography/countries/article/portugal
Learn more facts about Portugal.

Video

Portugal for Kids
www.youtube.com/watch?v=S-B4y_7kgjQ
Take a short virtual tour of Portugal.

Publisher's note to educators and parents: Our editors have carefully reviewed these websites to ensure that they are suitable for students. Many websites change frequently, however, and we cannot guarantee that a site's future contents will continue to meet our high standards of quality and educational value. Be advised that students should be closely supervised whenever they access the internet.

INDEX